HOME BAKINGS

Carole Handslip/Brian Binns

HAMLYN

CONTENTS

This edition prepared under the supervision of
Joanna Morris

This edition published in 1990 by
The Hamlyn Publishing Group Limited,
a division of the Octopus Publishing Group,
Michelin House, 81 Fulham Road,
London SW3 6RB

© 1980 Cathay Books

ISBN 0 600 56997 7

Produced by Mandarin Offset
Printed and Bound in Hong Kong

INTRODUCTION

Nothing establishes the reputation of the home cook more securely than her baked goods. And here is a collection of great reputation-makers. You'll find something for every occasion – snacking, rounding out meals, entertaining friends. And be you beginner or experienced baker, there's something perfect for you.

Perk up a meal of leftovers with freshly baked biscuits. Make an ordinary day special with a chocolate cream roll or a fresh blueberry or peach pie. Have the kids rush home from school for a taste of your gingerbread. And when it comes to a party, prepare a do-ahead cheesecake or the mocha Paris Brest and allow yourself the time to make the heart of the dinner as sensational as the end.

All of the recipes in this book are meant for enjoyment – the enjoyment of the baker and the enjoyment of those who share in the results.

NOTES

FLOUR: To measure, spoon lightly into the measuring cup, then level with a knife or spatula. Don't dip the measuring cup directly into the flour – it can result in heavy baked goods. Measure flour unsifted unless stated otherwise.

EGGS: All recipes have been tested with large eggs.

BUTTER: If possible, use unsalted butter for baking. The butter should be softened unless stated otherwise. Margarine may be substituted for butter.

VANILLA: Use pure vanilla extract, not imitation.

COCOA: Use unsweetened cocoa powder.

YEAST: Use active dry yeast.

TO LINE A BAKING PAN: Grease the pan with shortening, line the bottom with waxed paper and then grease the paper. Butter can be used only if unsalted.

FAMILY CAKES

Apple and Spice Cake

2 cups plus 2
  tablespoons
  all-purpose flour
1½ teaspoons
  baking powder
1½ teaspoons
  cinnamon
½ teaspoon salt
1 cup light brown
  sugar, packed
½ cup raisins
½ cup butter, melted
2 large eggs, lightly
  beaten
¾ cup milk
2 large tart apples,
  peeled and
  chopped
Powdered sugar

Sift the flour, baking powder, cinnamon and salt into a mixing bowl. Stir in the brown sugar and raisins. Mix in the melted butter, eggs, milk and apples and beat just until smooth.

Pour the batter into a greased and lined 8-inch square pan. Bake in a preheated 350° oven until the cake springs back when pressed lightly, 1 hour to 1 hour and 10 minutes.

Leave briefly in the pan; invert onto a rack to cool. Sprinkle with powdered sugar before serving.
Makes one 8-inch cake

Banana Cake

¾ cup butter
1 cup sugar
3 eggs
1 tablespoon yogurt
1 teaspoon vanilla
1½ cups all-purpose flour
1 teaspoon baking powder
½ teaspoon baking soda
Pinch of salt
2 medium ripe bananas, mashed
1 small ripe banana, chopped
¼ teaspoon fresh lemon juice
Quick Buttercream (page 93)
1 tablespoon rum
½ teaspoon vanilla

Cream the butter with the sugar until fluffy. Add the eggs one at a time; then the yogurt and vanilla. Sift the flour, baking powder, baking soda and salt. Fold into the batter just until blended; fold in the mashed bananas.

Pour the batter into a greased and floured 9-inch round layer pan. Bake in a preheated 350° oven until the cake springs back when pressed lightly, 35 to 40 minutes. Cool on a rack.

Toss the chopped banana with the lemon juice; stir in a third of the buttercream. Split the cake into 2 layers and use the mixture to sandwich them together. Flavor the remaining buttercream with the rum and vanilla and spread it over the top and side.

Makes one 9-inch layer cake

Carrot Cake

½ cup dark brown
   sugar, packed
6 tablespoons honey
2 cups finely grated
   carrots
1 cup raisins
½ cup golden raisins
½ cup butter
⅔ cup water
¾ teaspoon nutmeg
1 egg, lightly beaten
2 cups all-purpose
   flour
2 teaspoons baking
   powder
¼ teaspoon salt

Combine the sugar, honey, carrots, raisins, golden raisins, butter, water, and nutmeg in a saucepan. Bring to a boil; reduce the heat and simmer 5 minutes. Transfer the mixture to a bowl and cool to room temperature.

Stir in the egg. Sift together the flour, baking powder and salt and add to the bowl, stirring just until blended.

Pour the batter into a greased and floured 9 × 5-inch loaf pan. Bake in a preheated 350° oven until the center is set when pressed lightly, about 1 hour to 1 hour and 10 minutes. Invert onto a rack to cool.

Makes one 9-inch loaf

Coconut Loaf Cake

2 eggs
1 tablespoon milk
½ teaspoon vanilla
½ cup sugar
1 cup shredded
  coconut, lightly
  packed
1½ cups all-purpose
  flour
2 teaspoons baking
  powder
¼ teaspoon nutmeg
Pinch of salt
½ cup cold butter,
  cut up
TOPPING:
2 tablespoons
  shredded coconut
1 tablespoon sugar

Beat the eggs with the milk in a small mixing bowl; add the vanilla and stir in ¼ cup of the sugar and the coconut and allow to stand about 30 minutes.

Sift the flour, baking powder, nutmeg and salt into a bowl; stir in the remaining sugar. Cut in the butter until the mixture is crumbly. Add the coconut mixture and stir gently until well blended.

Pour the batter into a greased and floured 9 × 5-inch loaf pan. Mix together the coconut and sugar for the topping and scatter the mixture over the surface. Bake in a preheated 375° oven until the cake springs back when pressed lightly in the center, about 45 minutes. Invert onto a rack to cool.
Makes one 9-inch loaf

Devil's Food Cake

¾ cup cocoa
⅔ cup boiling water
1½ cups all-purpose
    flour
1 teaspoon baking
    soda
½ teaspoon baking
    powder
¼ teaspoon salt
½ cup butter
1¼ cups sugar
2 eggs, lightly beaten
CHOCOLATE
BUTTERCREAM:
6 oz semisweet
    chocolate, melted
    and cooled
Quick Buttercream
    (page 93)

Blend the cocoa with half of the boiling water until smooth; stir in remaining water and cool. Sift together the flour, baking soda, baking powder and salt; set aside.

Cream the butter and sugar until light; add 3 tablespoons of the cocoa mixture and beat until fluffy. Beat in the eggs, one at a time, beating thoroughly after each addition.

Alternately fold the dry ingredients and cocoa into the butter mixture. The mixture may be slightly curdled at this stage.

Divide the batter between two greased and lined 8-inch round layer pans. Bake in a preheated 350° oven until set in the center, about 30 minutes. Leave in the pans 5 minutes; invert onto a rack to cool.

Stir the melted chocolate into the buttercream. Sandwich the layers with part of the mixture. Frost the top and side of the cake with the remainder. Decorate with walnut halves if desired.

Makes one 9-inch layer cake

Chocolate Almond Cake

4 oz semisweet
   chocolate
½ cup butter
½ cup sugar
4 eggs, separated
1 teaspoon vanilla
¾ cup ground
   almonds
½ cup all-purpose
   flour
CHOCOLATE GLAZE:
6 oz semisweet
   chocolate
1 tablespoon strong
   coffee
2 tablespoons butter

Melt the chocolate over hot water. Cream the butter with the sugar until fluffy, then beat in the chocolate. Add the egg yolks, one at a time; add the vanilla, then beat in the almonds and flour until blended.

Beat the egg whites until stiff; gently fold them into the batter. Pour into a greased and lined 8-inch square pan. Bake in a preheated 325° oven until the center is set, about 1 hour. Leave in the pan for 5 minutes; invert onto a rack to cool.

Heat the glaze ingredients in the top of a double boiler until smooth. Cool slightly. Spread most of the glaze over the cake; leave until set. Decorate with the remaining glaze, using a pastry bag and plain tip.

Makes one 8-inch cake

11

Moist Gingerbread

2 cups all-purpose
   flour
1 tablespoon ginger
½ teaspoon
   cinnamon
¼ teaspoon each
   allspice and cloves
1 teaspoon baking
   soda
½ cup butter
1 cup molasses
¼ cup light brown
   sugar, packed
½ cup milk
2 eggs, beaten

Sift the flour, spices and baking soda
into a mixing bowl. Heat the butter,
molasses and brown sugar in a saucepan; cool slightly, then add to the dry
ingredients with the milk and eggs.
Mix thoroughly.

Pour the batter into a greased and
lined 8-inch square pan. Bake in a preheated 325° oven until set in the center, about 1 hour.

Leave in the pan for 15 minutes;
invert onto a rack to cool.

Makes one 8-inch cake

Glazed Fruitcake

2 cups all-purpose
  flour
½ teaspoon
  cinnamon
¼ teaspoon each
  allspice, nutmeg
  and cloves
¾ cup butter
¾ cup light brown
  sugar, packed
3 eggs
1 cup raisins
½ cup golden raisins
2 tablespoons
  chopped angelica
½ cup glacé cherries,
  quartered
2 tablespoons
  crystallized
  ginger, chopped
2 tablespoons
  dry sherry
APRICOT GLAZE:
2 tablespoons
  apricot jam
1 tablespoon water
Lemon juice

Grease a 7 or 8 × 3-inch round pan and line the base and side with foil. Tie a thick strip of brown wrapping paper around the outside of the pan and place on a baking sheet lined with brown paper.

Sift the flour with the spices. Cream the butter and sugar until fluffy. Beat in the eggs, one at a time, adding a spoonful of flour with the last two. Stir in the fruit, ginger and sherry; fold in the remaining flour.

Pour the batter into the pan and decorate with additional glacé fruit and walnuts. Bake in a preheated 325° oven for 1 hour; reduce the heat to 300° and bake until a pick inserted in the center comes out clean, about 1 hour. Leave in the pan for 5 minutes; invert onto a rack to cool.

Boil the apricot jam and water in a small saucepan for 3 minutes. Stir in a drop of lemon juice; strain and brush over the cake.

Makes one 7- or 8-inch cake

Caramel Crunch Cake

2 cups all-purpose
  flour
1 teaspoon baking
  powder
½ teaspoon baking
  soda
¼ teaspoon salt
½ cup butter
¾ cup light brown
  sugar, packed
3 eggs
¼ cup strong coffee
CARAMEL CRUNCH:
¾ cup sugar
3 tablespoons cold
  water
FILLING:
¼ cup butter
1 cup powdered
  sugar
2 tablespoons milk,
  or as needed
FROSTING:
Quick Buttercream
  (page 93)
1 teaspoon vanilla

Sift the flour, baking powder, baking soda and salt. Cream the butter and sugar until fluffy. Add the eggs, one at a time, adding a spoonful of flour with each egg. Add the coffee, then fold in the remaining flour.

Pour the batter into two greased and lined 8-inch round layer pans. Bake in a preheated 350° oven for 25 to 30 minutes. Leave in the pans for 5 minutes; invert onto a rack to cool.

For the caramel crunch, stir together the sugar and water in a small saucepan until dissolved. Bring to a boil and cook, without stirring, until the syrup turns medium amber. Immediately pour the boiling syrup onto a greased baking sheet and cool. When thoroughly cool and very hard, break the caramel into small pieces; crush half of the caramel with a rolling pin and reserve the remainder for decoration.

For the filling, cream together the butter and sugar; beat in the crushed caramel. Add enough milk for a spreadable consistency; use to sandwich the layers.

For the frosting, mix the buttercream and vanilla. Spread over the top and side of the cake; decorate with the caramel crunch.

Makes one 8-inch layer cake

Coffee Walnut Layer Cake

4 eggs
¾ cup sugar
1 cup all-purpose
   flour, sifted
1 tablespoon
   vegetable oil
1 cup (generous)
   finely chopped
   walnuts
COFFEE FROSTING:
1 tablespoon instant
   coffee, preferably
   espresso
1 tablespoon hot
   water
1½ recipes Quick
   Buttercream
   (page 93)

With an electric beater, beat the eggs and sugar in a bowl set over simmering water. When warm, remove from the heat; beat until very thick and tripled in volume.

Gently fold in the flour a little at a time; when almost incorporated, fold in the oil and nuts. Pour into two greased and lined 8-inch round layer pans. Bake in a preheated 375° oven until the cakes spring back when pressed, about 35 minutes. Invert onto a rack to cool; then split each cake horizontally with a serrated knife.

Dissolve the coffee in the hot water; stir into the buttercream. Spread a portion of the frosting onto three of the layers and sandwich the cake together. Swirl the remaining frosting on the top and side of the cake.

Makes one 8-inch layer cake

Date-Walnut Cake

½ cup dark brown
   sugar, packed
6 tablespoons honey
1½ cups chopped
   dates
½ cup butter
⅓ cup orange juice
⅓ cup water
½ teaspoon
   cinnamon
1 egg, lightly beaten
2 cups all-purpose
   flour
2 teaspoons baking
   powder
½ teaspoon baking
   soda
¼ teaspoon salt
1½ cups coarsely
   chopped walnuts

Combine the sugar, honey, dates, butter, orange juice, water and cinnamon
in a saucepan. Heat, stirring, until
blended. Transfer the mixture to a
mixing bowl and cool thoroughly.

Stir in the egg. Sift the flour, baking
powder, baking soda and salt; add to
the bowl, stirring just until blended.
Stir in the walnuts.

Pour the batter into a greased and
floured 9-inch round layer pan. Bake in
a preheated 350° oven until the center
is set when pressed lightly, about 1
hour to 1 hour and 10 minutes. Invert
onto a rack to cool.

Makes one 9-inch cake

Angel Food Cake

1 cup sifted cake
  flour
1½ cups sugar,
  preferably
  superfine
½ teaspoon salt
1½ cups egg whites,
  at room
  temperature
  (about 12 large)
1 teaspoon cream of
  tartar
1 tablespoon fresh
  lemon juice
1 teaspoon cold
  water
1½ teaspoons
  vanilla
¼ teaspoon almond
  extract

Sift the flour, ½ cup of the sugar and the salt onto a sheet of waxed paper. Sift the remaining cup of sugar onto another sheet and set aside. Sift the flour mixture 3 or 4 more times.

Beat the egg whites at medium-slow speed. When foamy, add the cream of tartar, lemon juice, water, vanilla and almond extract. Increase speed and beat until the whites form stiff peaks. Beat in the sugar, 2 tablespoons at a time, beating well after each addition. Sift and fold a quarter of the flour mixture at a time into the egg whites.

Pour the batter into a 10-inch angel food pan. Run a spatula through the mixture to eliminate any air pockets; smooth the top. Bake in a preheated 350° oven until cake springs back when pressed, about 45 minutes. Invert pan on a bottle until cool. If desired, frost with Quick Buttercream (page 93).
Makes one 10-inch cake

Jelly Roll

SPONGE CAKE:
4 eggs
¾ cup sugar
½ teaspoon vanilla
¾ cup sifted cake
   flour
FILLING:
½ cup raspberry jam,
   or more

Beat the eggs and sugar with an electric beater in a bowl set over simmering water. When warm, remove from heat; continue beating until the mixture is very thick and tripled in volume.

Stir in the vanilla; then gently fold in the flour, a third at a time. Pour the batter into a greased and lined 10 × 15-inch jelly-roll pan, smoothing it gently. Bake in a preheated 375° oven until pale gold and springy to the touch, 10 to 12 minutes.

Sprinkle a sheet of waxed paper with granulated sugar and place on a moist towel. Turn the cake out onto the paper and gently remove the lining paper. Spread the cake with jam and carefully roll up from a short edge, using the towel and waxed paper to help. Cool on a rack. Trim the edges.

Makes one cake roll

Chocolate Cream Roll

Sponge Cake
   (above)
¼ cup cocoa
FILLING:
1 cup heavy cream
2 tablespoons sugar
1 teaspoon vanilla
Cocoa

Prepare the sponge cake as directed, substituting the ¼ cup cocoa for ¼ cup of the cake flour, and sifting the cocoa and flour together.

After turning the cake onto the waxed paper, roll up and leave until cool. Whip the cream, sugar and vanilla until nearly stiff. Gently unroll the cake and spread with the whipped cream. Roll up again, trim the edges and sprinkle the cake with additional cocoa.

Makes one cake roll

Nut and Rum Ring

Sponge Cake (page 18)
¾ cup cold water
½ cup sugar
3 tablespoons rum
1 cup apricot preserves, strained
½ recipe Quick Buttercream (page 93)
½ cup each chopped hazelnuts and walnuts
Powdered sugar

Prepare the sponge cake as directed except bake in a greased and floured 9-inch tube or Bundt pan until set when pressed lightly, 30 to 35 minutes. Invert onto a rack to cool.

Heat the water and sugar in a saucepan, stirring, until the sugar has dissolved. Bring to a boil; boil 2 minutes. Remove from the heat, stir in the rum and leave to cool.

Split the cooled cake horizontally into 3 layers. Sprinkle each with the rum syrup and allow to absorb.

Spread the bottom layer with some of the preserves.

Place the second layer on top and spread with the buttercream. Place the remaining layer on top. Chill for 1 hour.

Place the cake on a rack placed over waxed paper. Bring the remaining apricot preserves to a boil and carefully pour over the cake to coat the surface. While the glaze is still warm and moist, sprinkle the nuts evenly over the cake. Dust the cake liberally with powdered sugar.

Makes one 9-inch tube cake

NOTE: Buttercream made with unsalted butter has a much fresher taste than that made with salted butter. For added flavor, stir rum into the apricot preserves.

Almond Cake

1 cup plus
   3 tablespoons
   butter
1 cup sugar
½ teaspoon almond
   extract
1 cup plus
   2 tablespoons
   ground almonds
Grated rind of ½
   lemon
3 eggs, beaten
1½ cups all-purpose
   flour
½ teaspoon salt
3 tablespoons sliced
   almonds

Cream the butter with the sugar until fluffy. Beat in the almond extract, ground almonds and lemon rind. Add the eggs, one at a time, beating well after each addition. Sift in the flour and salt, folding just until blended.

Pour the batter into a greased and floured 8-inch round layer pan and sprinkle with the sliced almonds. Sift powdered sugar over the almonds if desired.

Bake in a preheated 350° oven until set in the center, 45 to 50 minutes. Leave briefly in the pan; invert onto a rack to cool.

Makes one 8-inch cake

COMPANY CAKES

Sacher Torte

½ cup butter
½ cup sugar
3 tablespoons
   ground almonds
4 eggs, separated
1 teaspoon vanilla
6 oz semisweet
   chocolate, melted
   and cooled
1 cup all-purpose
   flour
¾ teaspoon baking
   powder
¼ teaspoon baking
   soda
Pinch of salt
¼ cup apricot
   preserves
Ganache (page 93)

Cream the butter with the sugar until fluffy. Beat in the ground almonds, egg yolks (one at a time), vanilla and chocolate. Sift the flour, baking powder, baking soda and salt; fold into the batter. Beat the egg whites to soft peaks; fold into the batter.

Pour the batter into a greased and floured 8-inch round layer pan. Bake in a preheated 350° oven until the center is firm to the touch, 45 to 55 minutes. After 5 minutes; invert onto a rack to cool.

Split the cake horizontally and sandwich the layers with the apricot preserves. Spread the warm ganache over the cake and leave to set.

Makes one 8-inch layer cake

Chocolate Truffle Cake

1⅓ cups all-purpose flour
1 cup cocoa
1½ teaspoons baking powder
¼ teaspoon salt
¾ cup sugar
½ cup butter, melted
2 eggs, beaten
6 tablespoons light corn syrup
⅔ cup milk
FROSTING:
½ recipe Quick Buttercream (page 93)
Ganache (page 93)
8 oz marzipan
2 oz semisweet chocolate, melted
2 tablespoons grated semisweet chocolate

Sift the dry ingredients into a bowl. Stir the remaining cake ingredients into the flour mixture.

Pour the batter into a greased and floured 9 × 5-inch loaf pan. Bake in a preheated 325° oven until the cake springs back when pressed lightly, 50 to 60 minutes. Leave briefly in the pan; invert onto a rack to cool. Trim and cut into 3 layers.

Mix the buttercream with half the ganache (chill the rest). Sandwich the layers with most of this mixture; smooth the remainder over the cake.

Roll out the marzipan thinly and cover the cake completely, pressing it gently onto the surface; trim off the excess. Chill the cake.

Drizzle the melted chocolate over the top of the cake. Form the remaining ganache into five to ten balls and roll in grated chocolate. Arrange on the cake.

10 servings

Caramel Dacquoise

4 egg whites
1 cup light brown
  sugar, packed
½ cup chopped
  toasted hazelnuts
  or almonds
1 cup heavy cream

Beat the egg whites until stiff but not dry. Gradually beat in the sugar. Use a pastry bag and ½-inch plain tip to pipe the meringue mixture onto two buttered and floured baking sheets. Begin in the center and form two neat 9-inch circles (press a cake pan into the flour as a guide). Sprinkle a small amount of the chopped nuts over one round.

Bake the meringues in a preheated 200° oven until crisp, about 2 hours. Cool the meringues briefly on the baking sheet; then carefully transfer to a rack to cool completely.

Whip the cream until almost stiff. Combine most of it with the remaining nuts and spread on the plain meringue. Top with the decorated meringue. Garnish with the remaining whipped cream and hazelnuts.

8 servings

Tia Maria Torte

¾ cup all-purpose
  flour
3 tablespoons cocoa
¾ teaspoon baking
  powder
¼ teaspoon baking
  soda
Pinch of salt
4 eggs, separated
⅓ cup sugar
¾ cup Sugar Syrup
  (page 93)
3 tablespoons Tia
  Maria
1 tablespoon strong
  coffee
Quick Buttercream
  (page 93)
Grated chocolate
12 small Florentines
  (page 37)

Sift the flour, cocoa, baking powder, baking soda and salt and set aside. Beat the egg yolks and sugar until light; fold in the dry ingredients. Beat the egg whites until stiff and carefully fold into the batter.

Pour the batter into two 9-inch round layer pans. Bake in a preheated 400° oven until the center springs back when lightly touched, 14 to 20 minutes. Invert onto a rack to cool.

Combine the sugar syrup and Tia Maria. Brush over the layers.

Stir the coffee into the buttercream and use a portion to sandwich the layers. Spread most of the remaining buttercream over the side and top of the cake. Gently coat the side with grated chocolate.

Using a pastry bag fitted with a star tip, pipe twelve rosettes onto the cake with the remaining buttercream. Top each with a florentine.

12 servings

Apricot Gâteau

Sponge Cake
(page 18)
1¼ cups heavy
cream
2 tablespoons sugar
½ teaspoon vanilla
¾ cup chopped
toasted almonds
⅔ cup apricot jam,
strained
1 can (17 oz) apricot
halves, well
drained

Prepare the sponge cake as directed except bake it in two greased and floured 8-inch round layer pans until set, about 30 minutes. Invert onto a rack to cool.

Whip the cream with the sugar and vanilla until nearly stiff; stir in about 2 tablespoons of the chopped almonds. Use part of the cream to sandwich the layers together. Brush the top of the cake with apricot jam; spread the remaining whipped cream over the side of the cake. Gently press the remaining chopped almonds onto the side of the cake.

Arrange the apricot halves over the top of the cake and brush them gently with the remaining apricot jam.

Makes one 8-inch layer cake

Chocolate Porcupine

Devil's Food Cake
    (page 10)
6 oz semisweet
    chocolate, melted
    and cooled
Quick Buttercream
    (page 93)
½ cup slivered
    almonds
3 jelly beans or other
    small candies

Prepare the devil's food cake as directed except bake it in one 9-inch round layer pan. Leave in the pan 5 minutes. Invert onto a rack to cool.

Stir the melted chocolate into the buttercream. Cut the cake in half to form two semicircles; sandwich the halves together with some of the frosting. Place the cake cut side down and form the nose by cutting a diagonal, pointed shape at one end of the cake; discard excess pieces. Cover the cake with the buttercream.

Smooth the frosting over the nose and face; fork lines from front to back over the rest of the "porcupine." Insert the slivered almonds along the back for the quills; position the jelly beans on the face to make the nose and eyes.
Makes one "porcupine"

Chocolate Dream Cake

3 eggs
½ cup sugar
½ cup all-purpose
   flour
⅓ cup cocoa
Chocolate
   Buttercream
   (page 10)
CHOCOLATE CURLS:
3 oz semisweet
   chocolate, melted

Beat the eggs and sugar over simmering water until warm. Remove from the heat and beat until the mixture is very thick. Sift the flour with the cocoa; fold into the batter. Pour into a greased and lined 9-inch round layer pan. Bake in a preheated 375° oven until set, 35 to 40 minutes. Invert onto a rack to cool.

For the chocolate curls, spread the melted chocolate on a baking sheet and leave until nearly set, but not too brittle. Use a sharp knife to shave off long chocolate curls, starting from the edge nearest to you.

Split the cake horizontally and sandwich the layers with some of the buttercream; use the rest on the top and side of the cake. Place the chocolate curls gently on the surface.

Makes one 9-inch cake

Gâteau Pithiviers

½ cup (generous) whole unblanched almonds
⅓ cup sugar
3 tablespoons butter
1 egg
½ teaspoon vanilla
½ teaspoon almond extract
3 tablespoons flour
1 package (17¼ oz) frozen puff pastry, thawed
GLAZE:
1 egg yolk, beaten with 2 teaspoons cold water
2 teaspoons sugar

In a blender, grind the almonds and sugar. In a bowl, mix with the butter, egg, vanilla and almond extract until smooth. Blend in the flour.

Roll out the puff pastry and cut out two 8-inch rounds, one slightly thicker than the other. Place the thinner round on a dampened baking sheet. Cover with the almond filling, leaving a 1-inch border around the edge. Dampen the pastry edges with cold water; place the thick round on top. Press the edges together; score at intervals with the back of a knife.

Cut a small hole in the center; score the pastry from the center to the edge. Brush with the egg, then sprinkle with the sugar. Bake in a preheated 425° oven until golden, about 30 minutes. Cool on a rack.

Makes one 8-inch cake

Hazelnut Meringue Cake

4 egg whites
1 cup sugar
1 cup hazelnuts,
    toasted, then
    ground with a
    little of the sugar
FILLING:
Double recipe
    Ganache (page 93)
GARNISH:
2 oz semisweet
    chocolate, melted
10 to 12 whole
    roasted hazelnuts

Beat the egg whites until almost stiff, then gradually beat in ½ cup of the sugar. Gently fold in the remaining sugar and the ground nuts.

Use a spatula to spread the meringue mixture into two even 9-inch circles on two greased and floured baking sheets (press a cake pan into the flour as a guide). Bake in a preheated 200° oven until crisp, 2 hours or longer. Cool briefly on the baking sheets, then carefully transfer the meringues to a rack to cool completely.

Whip the cooled ganache until just fluffy; do not overwhip. Use part of the ganache to sandwich the meringues together; spread part of the remaining ganache over the top and side. Drizzle the chocolate over the top of the cake, then pipe on the remaining ganache and top with the hazelnuts. This may be made a day ahead and refrigerated until ready to serve.

Makes one 9-inch cake

Mocha Paris Brest

CHOUX PASTRY:
1 cup water
6 tablespoons butter
⅔ cup all-purpose
  flour
Pinch of salt
½ teaspoon vanilla
4 eggs
½ cup sliced
  almonds

**FILLING AND
GARNISH:**
1 tablespoon strong
  coffee
3 tablespoons
  granulated sugar
1 tablespoon brandy
1¼ cups heavy
  cream, whipped
Powdered sugar

Heat the water and butter in a saucepan until boiling. Add the flour and salt; beat until the mixture comes together. Remove from the heat; add the vanilla and beat in the eggs, one egg at a time, reserving a spoonful of beaten egg.

Spoon the pastry into a 9-inch ring on a greased baking sheet. (Mark the circle with an inverted cake pan.) Brush with the reserved beaten egg and sprinkle with the almonds. Bake in a preheated 425° oven for 15 minutes; lower the heat to 375° and bake until golden, 25 minutes longer.

Split horizontally with a serrated knife. Scoop out any raw dough; return to the oven, cut sides up, for 5 minutes. Cool on a rack.

Beat the coffee, granulated sugar and brandy into the whipped cream and use to sandwich the cake. Sprinkle with the powdered sugar.

Makes one 9-inch cake

Ginger Cheesecake

CRUST:

1¼ cups graham
  cracker crumbs
  (16 squares)
6 tablespoons butter,
  melted

FILLING:

8 oz cottage cheese,
  sieved
2 tablespoons plain
  yogurt or sour
  cream
2 eggs, separated
2 tablespoons light
  brown sugar
2 tablespoons
  chopped preserved
  stem ginger or
  crystallized ginger
1 tablespoon ginger
  syrup (from jar)
Grated nutmeg

Combine the graham cracker crumbs and melted butter. Press onto the base and side of an 8- or 9-inch quiche pan. Set aside.

Blend the cottage cheese with the yogurt, egg yolks and sugar. Beat in the ginger and syrup. Beat the egg whites until stiff and fold into the cheese mixture. Pour into the pan and sprinkle with nutmeg.

Bake in a preheated 325° oven until lightly golden and firm, 25 to 30 minutes. Cool on a rack, then chill.

Serve garnished with whipped cream and sliced preserved ginger if desired.

Makes one 9-inch cheesecake

Orange Curaçao Cheesecake

CRUST:
- 1¼ cups graham cracker crumbs
- 6 tablespoons butter, melted
- ¼ cup brown sugar

FILLING:
- ¼ cup brown sugar
- 1 package (8 oz) cream cheese
- 8 oz cottage cheese, sieved
- 2 eggs, separated
- ½ cup sour cream
- 2 tablespoons granulated sugar
- Grated rind and juice of 1 orange
- 3 tablespoons Curaçao or Grand Marnier
- 1 envelope unflavored gelatin, softened in 2 tablespoons cold water

Stir together the graham cracker crumbs, melted butter and sugar. Press onto the bottom of an 8- or 9-inch springform pan and chill.

In a mixer bowl, beat the cream cheese with the cottage cheese until blended. Beat in the egg yolks, sour cream, granulated sugar, orange rind and juice and Curaçao. Dissolve the gelatin over low heat; stir into the mixture. Chill, stirring occasionally, until thick but not set. Beat the egg whites until stiff and fold into the cheese mixture. Pour into the pan and chill until firm. When firm, carefully remove the side of the pan.

Serve garnished with whipped cream and orange sections if desired.
Makes one 9-inch cheesecake

33

Marjolaine

An adaptation of the famous cake created by the late Chef Fernand Point at La Pyramide in Vienne, France.

CAKE LAYERS:
1 cup hazelnuts
1 cup (generous) sliced almonds
1 cup sugar
1 tablespoon flour
6 egg whites

CHOCOLATE CREAM:
4 oz semisweet chocolate, cut up
1 cup heavy cream

ORANGE CREAM:
½ cup butter
½ cup heavy cream
2 tablespoons sugar
Grated rind of ½ orange

Grind the hazelnuts, almonds and sugar in a blender or food processor until powdery. Stir in the flour. Beat the egg whites until stiff. Fold the nut mixture into the whites.

Gently pour the batter into a greased and lined 10 × 15-inch jelly-roll pan and spread it out to the edges with a spatula. Bake in a preheated 400° oven until golden, about 10 minutes. Cool briefly, then run a knife around the edges and invert onto a rack. Peel off the lining paper and cool.

For the chocolate cream, heat the chocolate and cream in a saucepan until smooth. Chill until cold. Whip until fluffy (do not overbeat).

For the orange cream, beat the butter until fluffy. Whip the cream and sugar until very thick, then fold into the butter gradually. Fold in the orange rind.

Trim the edges of the cake and cut into three lengthwise strips. Place one strip on a long board and spread with the chocolate cream. Top with another cake strip; chill until set. Spread with half of the orange cream and top with the remaining strip of cake.

Cover the top and sides with a smooth layer of orange cream. Chill for at least 1 hour. Serve sprinkled with powdered sugar.

10 servings

COOKIES & SMALL PASTRIES

Chocolate Chip Blondies

¼ cup butter, melted
1 cup brown sugar, packed
1 egg, lightly beaten
1 teaspoon vanilla
½ cup sifted all-purpose flour
1 teaspoon baking powder
¼ teaspoon salt
½ cup chopped pecans or walnuts
½ cup semisweet chocolate chips

Stir together the melted butter and brown sugar; then stir in the egg and vanilla. Sift the flour, baking powder and salt into the butter mixture and stir. Gently fold in the nuts and chocolate chips.

Pour the batter into a greased 8-inch square pan. Bake in a preheated 350° oven until set but still soft, about 25 minutes. Cool in the pan; then cut into bars.

Makes 16 bars

Florentines

¼ cup butter

3 tablespoons dark brown sugar

3 tablespoons corn syrup

¾ cup sliced almonds

¼ cup chopped dates

½ cup all-purpose flour

Grated rind of ½ lemon and ½ orange

1 teaspoon lemon juice

5 oz semisweet chocolate, melted

In a small saucepan, combine the butter, sugar and syrup. Bring to a boil, stirring; remove from the heat. Mix in the remaining ingredients except the chocolate, and let cool.

Drop 3-tablespoon mounds of the mixture onto lined baking sheets, spacing the mounds well apart. Use a wet fork to spread into 3-inch rounds. Bake in a preheated 350° oven until golden brown, about 8 to 10 minutes. Cool on the sheets for about a minute, then transfer to a rack until cool.

Spread the chocolate on the flat side of each cookie; let dry, chocolate side up. Store covered in a cool place.

Makes 18 to 20 cookies

Almond Tuiles

1 cup butter
½ cup sugar
2 egg whites
½ teaspoon vanilla
½ cup ground
  almonds
½ cup all-purpose
  flour
⅓ cup chopped
  almonds

Cream the butter and sugar until light; add the egg whites and vanilla. Gently stir in the ground almonds and flour.

Drop by teaspoonfuls, well apart, onto a greased and floured baking sheet. Flatten the cookies slightly with the back of a damp spoon. Sprinkle with the chopped nuts.

Bake in a preheated 350° oven until golden, 8 to 10 minutes. Leave on the baking sheet for 1 minute, then cool wrapped on a rolling pin. Leave until set, then remove.

Makes about 2 dozen

Ladyfingers

2 eggs
¼ cup granulated
  sugar
½ teaspoon vanilla
½ cup all-purpose
  flour, sifted
Powdered sugar

Beat the eggs and granulated sugar in a mixing bowl set over a pan of hot water. When the mixture is thick, remove from the heat and fold in the vanilla and flour.

Place the mixture in a pastry bag with a ½-inch plain tip and pipe into finger lengths on two greased and floured baking sheets. Sprinkle with powdered sugar. Bake in a preheated 375° oven until golden, 10 to 12 minutes. Transfer to a rack to cool.

Makes about 12 ladyfingers

Chocolate Truffles

Ganache (page 93)
Cocoa
Grated semisweet
  chocolate

Cool the ganache until firm but still malleable. Form into walnut-size balls and roll each truffle carefully in either cocoa or grated chocolate. Chill.

Makes about 3 dozen truffles

Crunchy Oatmeal Wafers

1¾ cups rolled oats (not instant)
¼ cup flour
1 cup light brown sugar, packed
Pinch of salt
½ cup vegetable oil
1 egg, lightly beaten
½ teaspoon almond extract
¼ teaspoon vanilla

Place the oats, flour, brown sugar and salt in a mixing bowl and stir to combine. Add the oil, egg and extracts and beat to combine thoroughly. Place teaspoonfuls of dough well apart on two greased baking sheets; press flat with a damp fork.

Bake in a preheated 325° oven until golden, 10 to 15 minutes. Cool briefly on the sheets, then transfer to a rack to cool completely.

Makes about 30 cookies

Oatmeal Bars

½ cup butter
¾ cup dark brown
   sugar, packed
¼ cup light corn
   syrup
½ teaspoon vanilla
3½ cups rolled oats
   (not instant)
Pinch of salt

Melt the butter in a saucepan with the sugar and syrup, stirring. Remove from the heat and stir in vanilla, oats and salt. Transfer the mixture to a greased 8-inch square pan and smooth the top.

Bake in a preheated 350° oven until golden, about 25 minutes. Cool in the pan for about 5 minutes, then cut into bars with a sharp knife. Cool completely before removing the bars from the pan.

Makes 16 bars

Frangipane Tarts

½ package (17¼-oz size) frozen puff pastry, thawed
3 tablespoons butter
¼ cup sugar
Finely grated rind of 1 lemon
1 egg, beaten
6 tablespoons ground almonds
1 tablespoon heavy cream
Raspberry jam

Roll out the pastry thinly on a lightly floured surface and prick all over with a fork. Cut out twelve 2½-inch circles. Fit the pastry into muffin or small tart pans.

Cream the butter and sugar; add the lemon rind and egg. Mix in the almonds and cream until smooth.

Place about ¼ teaspoon raspberry jam in each tart shell. Cover with the almond mixture to fill the shells three-quarters full. Bake in a preheated 375° oven until golden, about 15 to 20 minutes. Cool on a rack.

Makes 12 tarts

Macaroon Tartlets

½ package (17¼-oz size) frozen puff pastry, thawed, or double recipe Rich Tart Pastry (page 92)

2 tablespoons raspberry jam, or more as needed

⅔ cup ground almonds

¾ cup sugar

3 egg whites, or more as needed

Roll out the pastry thinly on a lightly floured surface and prick all over with a fork. Cut out eighteen 2½-inch circles, reserving the pastry trimmings. Fit the pastry circles into muffin or small tart pans and place a small dab of jam in each pastry shell.

Mix together the ground almonds and sugar. Add the egg whites and beat with a wooden spoon for about 3 minutes; the mixture should be quite fluid. Beat in a bit more egg white if necessary. Fill each shell three-quarters full.

Cut the pastry trimmings into strips ¼ × 2½ inches. Place them crosswise on top of the filling and let stand a few minutes.

Bake in a preheated 350° oven until golden, about 25 minutes. Cool on a rack.

Makes 18 tarts

Almond Macaroons

1 cup sugar
1 cup ground
  almonds
1 tablespoon
  cornstarch
2 egg whites
25 almond halves

Mix the sugar, ground almonds and cornstarch and set aside. Beat the egg whites lightly; add the dry ingredients and beat until smooth.

Let stand for 5 minutes, then roll into small balls and place on a greased and floured baking sheet, spacing the balls slightly. Flatten gently and place an almond half on each cookie.

Bake in a preheated 350° oven until lightly golden, about 15 minutes. Cool on the baking sheet.
Makes about 25 cookies

Nut Galettes

½ cup butter
⅓ cup sugar
1 egg yolk
½ cup ground almonds
1½ cups all-purpose flour
1 to 2 teaspoons milk, as needed
TOPPING:
1 cup powdered sugar, sifted
1 egg white
¼ teaspoon almond extract
½ cup slivered almonds

Cream the butter and sugar until light; then add the egg yolk. Add the ground almonds and flour and knead until blended. Knead in enough milk to make a cohesive dough.

Roll out the dough to ¼-inch thickness. Cut into 2½-inch rounds and transfer to two greased baking sheets.

Stir together the topping ingredients and spoon over the cookies. Bake in a preheated 350° oven until golden, 10 to 15 minutes. Cool on a rack.

Makes 24 to 28 cookies

Date and Oat Bars

1 cup chopped dates
2 tablespoons water
1 tablespoon lemon
  juice
1 tablespoon honey
1½ cups all-purpose
  flour
2½ cups rolled oats
  (not instant)
¾ cup cold butter,
  cut up
¼ cup light brown
  sugar

In a small saucepan, simmer the dates, water, lemon juice and honey until the dates are soft. Let cool.

Meanwhile, mix the flour and oats together; then cut in the butter until crumbly. Stir in the brown sugar.

Firmly press half of the oat mixture into the bottom of a greased 8-inch square pan. Cover completely with the date mixture. Sprinkle the remaining oat mixture on top and press gently with your fingertips.

Bake in a preheated 375° oven until golden, 25 to 35 minutes. While still warm, cut into bars. Cool in the pan before removing.

Makes 16 bars

Butter Shortbread

¾ cup butter
¼ cup sugar
1½ cups all-purpose
   flour

Cream the butter and sugar together until light and fluffy. Sift in the flour and stir just until the dough holds together.

Place the dough on a lightly floured board and knead until smooth. Roll out into an 8-inch circle and place on a greased baking sheet. Pinch all around the edge, prick with a fork and mark into wedges. Sprinkle with additional sugar.

Bake in a preheated 325° oven until pale golden, about 30 to 40 minutes. Leave on the baking sheet for 5 minutes, then transfer carefully to a rack to cool completely.

Makes one 8-inch round

Chocolate Caramel Bars

PASTRY:
½ cup butter
¼ cup sugar
1½ cups all-purpose
    flour, sifted
CARAMEL FILLING:
½ cup butter
¼ cup sugar
⅓ cup sweetened
    condensed milk
2 tablespoons light
    corn syrup
1 teaspoon vanilla
CHOCOLATE
TOPPING:
4 oz semisweet
    chocolate, melted
    with 1 tablespoon
    butter

For the pastry, cream the butter and sugar until fluffy. Add the flour. Press evenly into an 8-inch square pan and prick with a fork. Bake in a preheated 350° oven until pale gold and baked through, 12 to 15 minutes.

For the filling, stir the butter, sugar, condensed milk and corn syrup over medium heat until dissolved. Bring to a boil, then simmer 5 to 7 minutes. Add the vanilla and spread over the pastry; allow to set.

Spread the chocolate topping over the filling and allow to set. Cut into bars.

Makes 16 bars

Almond Bars

Rich Tart Pastry
   (page 92)
¼ cup raspberry jam
1 cup sugar
1 cup plus
   2 tablespoons
   ground almonds
2 tablespoons
   cornstarch
3 eggs, lightly beaten
¼ cup sliced
   almonds

Roll out the pastry thinly on a lightly floured surface and fit it into a 9-inch square pan, trimming any excess. Spread the jam evenly over the pastry.

In a bowl, mix together the sugar, ground almonds and cornstarch, then add the eggs. Beat until the mixture is smooth and creamy. Spoon onto the jam, spreading it evenly. Sprinkle with the sliced almonds.

Bake in a preheated 400° oven until golden, about 20 minutes. Cool slightly, then cut into bars. Leave in the pan until cool.

Makes 18 bars

Honey and Almond Tarts

Double recipe
  Rich Tart Pastry
  (page 92)
¼ cup butter
¼ cup sugar
3 tablespoons honey
2 tablespoons heavy
  cream
¾ cup sliced
  almonds
½ teaspoon vanilla

Roll out the pastry thinly on a lightly floured surface and cut out eighteen 2½-inch circles. Fit the pastry into muffin or small tart pans.

Place the butter, sugar and honey in a heavy saucepan and heat gently until melted. Add the cream and bring to a boil; remove from the heat and stir in the almonds and vanilla. Cool, then spoon the mixture into the pastry shells.

Bake in a preheated 400° oven until lightly golden, 15 to 20 minutes. Cool the tarts on a rack and serve at room temperature.
Makes about 18 tarts

Cheesecake Tartlets

Double recipe
  Rich Tart Pastry
  (page 92)
¼ cup butter
¼ cup sugar
2 tablespoons fresh
  bread crumbs
½ teaspoon nutmeg
Pinch of salt
2 eggs, lightly beaten
8 oz cottage cheese,
  sieved
Juice of ½ lemon
½ teaspoon vanilla
¼ cup dried currants

Roll out the pastry thinly on a lightly floured surface and cut out eighteen 2½-inch circles. Fit the pastry into muffin or small tart pans.

Mix together the butter, sugar, bread crumbs, nutmeg and salt. Stir in the eggs and cheese, mixing well. Then stir in lemon juice, vanilla and currants. Spoon the mixture into the pastry shells. Bake in a preheated 375° oven until the filling is set, 20 to 25 minutes. Cool on a rack and serve at room temperature.

Makes 18 tarts

51

Gingersnaps

2 cups all-purpose
  flour
1 tablespoon ginger,
  or to taste
1½ teaspoons
  baking powder
¼ teaspoon baking
  soda
Pinch of salt
6 tablespoons cold
  butter
½ cup light brown
  sugar, packed
½ cup light corn
  syrup
2 tablespoons milk
½ teaspoon vanilla

Sift the flour, ginger, baking powder, baking soda and salt into a mixing bowl. Cut in the butter until crumbled; then stir in the sugar.

Stir together the corn syrup, milk and vanilla and add to the flour mixture. Knead lightly and shape into a long roll about 1½ inches in diameter. Wrap in plastic wrap and chill.

Cut the dough into ¼-inch slices and place about ½ inch apart on two greased baking sheets. Bake in a preheated 350° oven until the tops are crackled and golden, 10 to 15 minutes. Allow to cool on the sheets 2 minutes; then transfer to a rack to cool.

Makes about 3 dozen cookies

Almond Shortbreads

1 cup butter
1¾ cups all-purpose
  flour, sifted
½ cup ground
  almonds
½ cup sugar
12 almonds, halved

Place the butter, flour, ground almonds and sugar in a bowl and mix together to form a smooth dough. Shape into a rectangular log about 6 inches long, 3 inches wide and 1¼ inches high. Chill for at least 1 hour.

Cut the dough into ¼-inch slices and place well apart on greased baking sheets. Press a halved almond into the center of each cookie. Bake in a preheated 275° oven until pale golden, 25 to 35 minutes. Cool on a rack.

Makes about 2 dozen cookies

Coconut Macaroons

2½ cups shredded
   coconut (about
   8 oz)
1¼ cups sugar
5 egg whites
9 glacé cherries,
   halved

Stir together the coconut and sugar.
Beat the egg whites until frothy and
mix with the coconut. Chill briefly.

Divide the mixture into 18 mounds
on a greased and floured baking sheet.
Top each mound with half a glacé
cherry. Bake in a preheated 350° oven
until pale gold, about 15 to 20 minutes.
Cool on a rack.

Makes about 18 cookies

Almond Crunch Tartlets

Rich Tart Pastry
  (page 92)
¼ cup butter
¼ cup sugar
1 egg, lightly beaten
1 tablespoon flour
2¼ cups ground
  almonds
¼ teaspoon almond
  extract
¼ cup sliced
  almonds
2 tablespoons
  strained apricot
  preserves

Roll out the pastry thinly on a lightly floured surface and cut out ten 3-inch circles. Use to line 10 small tart pans. Trim the excess dough by pressing the rolling pin across the top of each tartlet pan. Chill the pastry-lined pans for about 15 minutes.

Cream the butter and sugar together until light and fluffy; add the egg, then beat in the flour. Mix in the ground almonds and extract.

Spoon the filling into the pastry shells, or pipe in with a pastry bag fitted with a ½-inch plain tip. Fill the shells two-thirds full. Sprinkle with sliced almonds.

Bake in a preheated 400° oven until golden, about 20 minutes. Transfer to a rack, then brush with the strained apricot preserves. Remove from the pans to serve.

Makes 10 tarts

Brandy Snaps

½ cup butter
½ cup light brown sugar, packed
½ cup light corn syrup
1 cup all-purpose flour
1 teaspoon ginger

Gently heat the butter, sugar and syrup in a saucepan, stirring, until the butter has melted and the sugar has dissolved. Cool slightly, then sift in the flour and ginger and stir until blended.

Place teaspoonfuls of the mixture at least 4 inches apart on a greased baking sheet. Bake in a preheated 350° oven until golden, about 10 minutes.

Cool slightly. While still warm, remove the cookies with a spatula and roll around the oiled handle of a wooden spoon or rolling pin. Allow to set for 1 to 2 minutes, then slip the cookies onto a rack to cool. Serve plain or filled with whipped cream.

Makes about 3 dozen cookies

Apple Turnovers

½ package (17¼-oz size) frozen puff pastry, thawed

3 medium tart apples, peeled and finely diced

1 teaspoon lemon juice

1 tablespoon sugar

¼ teaspoon vanilla

Roll out the pastry on a lightly floured surface to ⅛-inch thickness. Cut out as many 4-inch rounds as possible. Press the trimmings together and roll out again. Roll the rounds slightly across the center to make them oval.

Stir together the apples, lemon juice, sugar and vanilla. Place a tablespoon of the mixture in the center of each pastry round. Dampen the edges with cold water and fold over to make half-circles; seal. Brush lightly with water and sprinkle with additional sugar.

Place on baking sheets and bake in a preheated 425° oven until golden brown, about 15 minutes. Transfer to a rack and allow to cool. If desired, gently split each turnover at the seam, and pipe in whipped cream.

Makes about 10 turnovers

Currant Buns

½ package (17¼-oz size) frozen puff pastry, thawed, or Rich Tart Pastry (page 92)
½ cup dried currants
2 tablespoons light brown sugar
2 tablespoons butter, melted
Granulated sugar

Roll out the pastry on a lightly floured surface and cut out as many 4-inch rounds as possible. Dampen the edge of each round with cold water.

Mix the currants, brown sugar and butter and place a heaping teaspoon of the mixture in the middle of each pastry round. Fold the outer edge of the pastry in toward the center, pinch gently to seal and flatten slightly. Invert each round, seam side down, on a buttered baking sheet, and flatten each bun into a neat round shape. Make three small slits in the top of each bun.

Brush the pastry lightly with cold water and sprinkle with granulated sugar. Bake in a preheated 425° oven until golden brown, about 15 to 20 minutes. Cool on a rack.
Makes about 10 buns

Ginger Sponge Bars

1½ cups all-purpose
flour
1 tablespoon ginger
1 teaspoon baking
powder
¼ teaspoon salt
½ cup plus 2
tablespoons cold
butter
½ cup light corn
syrup
⅓ cup light brown
sugar, packed
3 eggs, lightly beaten
3 tablespoons sliced
almonds

Sift the flour, ginger, baking powder and salt into a large bowl; cut in the butter until crumbly.

Stir in the syrup, sugar and eggs, beating well until the batter is smooth and creamy, about 2 minutes.

Pour the batter into a greased and floured 8-inch square pan; sprinkle the almonds over the top. Bake in a preheated 350° oven until set in the center, about 30 minutes. Invert onto a rack to cool. Cut into slices.

Makes about 16 bars

Dutch Honey Squares

1½ cups all-purpose
flour
1½ teaspoons
cinnamon
1½ teaspoons
baking powder
¼ teaspoon salt
½ cup plus 2
tablespoons
butter, melted
½ cup honey
⅓ cup light brown
sugar, packed
1 egg, lightly beaten
1 egg yolk
3 tablespoons milk
⅓ cup sliced
almonds

Sift the flour, cinnamon, baking powder and salt into a large bowl. Stir in the butter, honey, sugar, egg, egg yolk and milk and beat until smooth, about 2 minutes.

Pour the batter into a greased and floured 8-inch square pan and sprinkle sliced almonds over the top. Bake in a preheated 350° oven until set, about 25 to 30 minutes. Invert onto a rack to cool. Cut into squares to serve.

Makes about 16 squares

Orange Spice Cakes

1½ cups all-purpose
flour
1½ teaspoons
baking powder
1 teaspoon nutmeg
¼ teaspoon salt
½ cup plus
2 tablespoons
butter, melted
⅓ cup bitter orange
marmalade
⅓ cup light brown
sugar, packed
2 eggs, beaten
1 tablespoon milk

Sift the flour, baking powder, nutmeg and salt into a bowl. Stir in the butter, marmalade, sugar, eggs and milk and mix thoroughly, until smooth and creamy.

Pour the batter into a greased and floured 8-inch square pan. Bake in a preheated 350° oven until set in the center, about 30 to 35 minutes. Invert onto a rack to cool. Cut into bars to serve.

Makes about 16 slices

TARTS & PIES

Pear Custard Tart

Rich Tart Pastry
(page 92)
2 ripe pears, peeled
and thinly sliced
CUSTARD:
½ cup heavy cream
½ cup milk
1 egg
1 egg yolk
3 tablespoons sugar
¼ teaspoon nutmeg
½ teaspoon vanilla

Roll out the pastry on a lightly floured surface and fit into a 9-inch quiche pan with a removable bottom. Place the pan on a baking sheet, line the pastry with foil and fill with dried beans. Bake in a preheated 400° oven for 8 minutes. Remove the foil and beans; prick the pastry with a fork and bake until very pale gold, another 5 minutes.

Arrange the pear slices over the pastry, overlapping slightly. Beat together the custard ingredients and pour over the pears. Bake until the custard has set, about 25 minutes. Serve warm or at room temperature.

Makes one 9-inch tart

Tarte Amandine

Rich Tart Pastry
  (page 92)
½ cup butter
½ cup sugar
3 eggs
¾ cup ground
  almonds
3 tablespoons
  raspberry
  preserves
TOPPING:
½ cup powdered
  sugar, sifted
1 to 2 teaspoons
  brandy or water
¼ cup sliced
  almonds

Roll out the pastry on a lightly floured surface and fit into a 9-inch quiche pan with a removable bottom. Place the pan on a baking sheet, line the pastry with foil and fill with dried beans. Bake in a preheated 400° oven for 8 minutes. Remove the foil and beans; prick the pastry and bake 5 minutes. Remove from the oven; lower the heat to 350°.

Beat the butter and sugar until fluffy. Beat in the eggs one at a time. Stir in the ground almonds.

Spread the preserves over the pastry and cover with the almond mixture. Bake until the center is set when lightly pressed, 30 to 35 minutes.

Mix the powdered sugar with enough brandy to be of thin pouring consistency; spread over the hot tart. Sprinkle with sliced almonds and bake 5 minutes.

Makes one 9-inch tart

Southern Pecan Pie

Basic Pie Pastry
(page 92)
3 eggs
1 cup light corn
 syrup
1 cup dark brown
 sugar, packed
3 tablespoons butter,
 melted
1 teaspoon vanilla
Pinch each of
 cinnamon and salt
2 cups pecans
Whipped cream

Roll out the pastry and use it to line a 10-inch pie plate; flute the edge. Chill the pastry.

Beat the eggs with the corn syrup, sugar, butter, vanilla, cinnamon and salt until the mixture is smooth. Stir in half of the pecans and pour the mixture into the pie shell. Arrange the remaining pecans over the surface.

Bake in a preheated 400° oven for 15 minutes; lower the heat to 350° and bake until set, about 35 minutes more. Cool on a rack; serve warm or at room temperature with whipped cream.
Makes one 10-inch pie

Baked Custard Tart

Basic Pie Pastry
(page 92)
4 eggs
3 tablespoons sugar
2 cups milk
1 teaspoon vanilla
Grated nutmeg

Roll out the pastry on a lightly floured surface and fit into a 9-inch tart pan. Line the pastry with foil and fill with dried beans. Bake in a preheated 400° oven for 8 minutes. Remove the foil and beans; prick the pastry with a fork and bake 6 minutes longer. Remove from the oven and lower the heat to 325°.

Beat together the eggs, sugar, milk and vanilla; strain into the pastry shell and sprinkle with nutmeg.

Bake until set, about 30 to 35 minutes. Serve warm or let cool to room temperature.
Makes one 9-inch tart

Cream Puffs

Choux Pastry
(page 31)
Pastry Cream
(page 92)
½ cup heavy cream,
    whipped
Powdered sugar

Prepare the choux pastry as directed. Spoon 2-inch rounds of the pastry dough onto a greased and floured baking sheet.

Bake in a preheated 400° oven for 20 minutes; lower the heat to 300° and continue to bake until the puffs are golden brown and dry, about 10 to 15 minutes. Remove from the oven, slice each puff horizontally with a serrated knife and cool completely.

Fold together the pastry cream and whipped cream and spoon into the cooled puffs. Replace the tops and serve sprinkled with powdered sugar.
Makes 12 to 16 puffs

Tarte à l'Orange

Rich Tart Pastry
    (page 92)
1¼ cups milk
3 egg yolks
½ cup sugar
¼ cup flour
1 teaspoon vanilla
1 tablespoon butter
3 oranges, peeled and
    sliced
½ cup orange
    marmalade,
    melted and
    strained

Roll out the pastry on a lightly floured surface and fit into a 9-inch tart pan. Place the pan on a baking sheet, line the pastry with foil and fill with dried beans. Bake in a preheated 400° oven for 8 minutes. Remove the foil and beans; prick the pastry with a fork and continue to bake until golden, about 10 minutes. Cool.

Bring the milk to a boil. Meanwhile, in a bowl, beat together the egg yolks, sugar and flour. Gradually beat the hot milk into the mixture. Return the mixture to the pan and bring to a boil, beating. Boil 1 minute; strain into a bowl and stir in the vanilla and butter. Place a piece of plastic wrap on the custard surface and cool.

Spread the custard over the pastry evenly. Arrange the orange slices, overlapping, over the custard and brush with the marmalade. Chill for 1 hour before serving.
Makes one 9-inch tart

Fresh Peach Pie

Double recipe
  Basic Pie Pastry
  (page 92)
6 large peaches
2 teaspoons lemon
  juice
½ cup brown sugar,
  packed
2 tablespoons
  granulated sugar
2 tablespoons
  cornstarch
Pinch each nutmeg
  and salt
1 tablespoon cold
  butter, cut into
  bits

Divide the pastry into two slightly unequal portions. Roll out the larger portion and fit into a 10-inch pie plate. Roll out the remaining pastry into a larger round and set aside.

Peel the peaches by dipping them briefly into boiling water, then slipping off their skins with a paring knife. Slice the peaches into a mixing bowl, tossing them with the lemon juice.

Sift together the sugars, cornstarch, nutmeg and salt. Toss gently with the peaches, then transfer to the pie dish, mounding slightly in the center. Dot with butter and top with the remaining pastry; seal and flute. Brush lightly with water, then sprinkle with additional granulated sugar. Cut several vents in the top crust.

Bake in a preheated 425° oven until golden, about 45 minutes. Cool on a rack and serve warm or at room temperature.

Makes one 10-inch pie

Fresh Blueberry Pie

Double recipe
  Basic Pie Pastry
  (page 92)
5 cups blueberries
2 teaspoons lemon
  juice
1 cup sugar
3 tablespoons
  cornstarch
Pinch of cinnamon
1 tablespoon cold
  butter, cut into
  bits

Divide the pastry into two slightly unequal portions. Roll out the larger portion and fit into a 10-inch pie plate. Roll out the remaining pastry into a larger round and set aside.

Toss the berries with the lemon juice in a large bowl. In a separate bowl, mix the sugar, cornstarch and cinnamon; toss this mixture with the berries and transfer to the pie plate. Dot with butter and fit the top crust over; seal and flute. Brush the pastry with cream and sprinkle with additional sugar. Cut several vents in the top crust.

Bake in a preheated 425° oven until the pie is golden brown and the filling is bubbly, about 45 minutes. Serve warm, with scoops of vanilla ice cream if desired.

Makes one 10-inch pie

Royal Cheese Tart

Rich Tart Pastry or
  Basic Pie Pastry
  (page 92)
8 oz cottage cheese,
  sieved
½ cup ground
  almonds
¼ cup sugar
2 eggs, separated
Grated rind and juice
  of 1 lemon
1 teaspoon vanilla
¼ cup golden raisins
⅔ cup heavy cream

Roll out the pastry on a lightly floured surface and fit into a 9-inch tart pan. Place the pan on a baking sheet and prick the pastry with a fork.

Combine the cheese, almonds, sugar, egg yolks, lemon rind and juice and vanilla in a bowl, beating until smooth. Stir in the raisins and cream. Beat the egg whites until stiff and fold into the cheese mixture. Pour into the pastry shell and bake in a preheated 400° oven for 20 minutes. Lower the heat to 350° and bake until the tart is firm and golden, about 15 to 20 minutes longer. Cool on a rack.

Serve warm or cool, sprinkled with powdered sugar if desired.
Makes one 9-inch tart

Apple Streusel Pie

Basic Pie Pastry or
Rich Tart Pastry
(page 92)
1½ lb apples, peeled
and sliced
¼ cup raisins
Grated rind of ½
lemon
¾ cup all-purpose
flour
⅓ cup sugar
1 teaspoon
cinnamon
3 tablespoons cold
butter, cut into
small bits
1 cup heavy cream
Cinnamon sugar

Roll out the pastry on a lightly floured surface and fit into a 10-inch quiche pan. Line the pastry with foil and fill with dried beans. Bake in a preheated 400° oven until the side has set, about 5 minutes. Remove the foil and beans; prick the pastry with a fork and bake for a further 5 minutes, when it should be cooked.

Mix the apples, raisins and lemon rind. Combine the flour, sugar and cinnamon in a bowl; cut in the butter until crumbly. Sprinkle half of the flour mixture into the pastry shell. Top with the apple mixture, pour in the cream and then top with the remaining flour mixture.

Sprinkle the cinnamon sugar over the pie and dot with additional bits of butter. Bake for 25 minutes; lower the heat to 375° and bake until bubbly, 10 to 15 minutes.
Makes one 10-inch pie

Linzer Torte

PASTRY:
½ cup butter
1½ cups powdered
 sugar, sifted
1 egg, lightly beaten
Grated rind of 1
 lemon
¾ cup ground
 almonds,
 hazelnuts or a
 combination
1 cup all-purpose
 flour, sifted
TOPPING AND
GLAZE:
¼ cup raspberry
 preserves
2 tablespoons
 apricot jam,
 melted and
 strained

Cream the butter and powdered sugar until fluffy, then beat in the egg and lemon rind. Stir together the nuts and flour and add to the butter, mixing just until the mixture forms a smooth, pliable dough. Form into a ball, wrap in plastic wrap and chill for 1 hour. (This dough also freezes well.)

Grease a 9-inch quiche pan with a removable bottom. Carefully roll out the dough on a lightly floured surface to a neat ¼-inch-thick round. Slide the bottom of the tart pan under the dough. Trim the dough around the bottom and reserve. Place the pastry-covered bottom inside the pan. Spread with the preserves, leaving a 1-inch border all around.

Gather the dough trimmings and roll out to ⅛-inch thickness, then cut into ½-inch-wide strips; reserve the excess. Lay the strips carefully over the preserves in a lattice pattern. Shape the remaining dough into a rope and fit it neatly onto the pastry border. Press into position with a fork, forming a neat edge.

Bake in a preheated 375° oven until golden, about 20 to 25 minutes. Cool in the pan on a rack, then brush the pastry lattice with warm apricot jam.
Makes one 9-inch torte

Lemon Curd Tartlets

Linzer Pastry
  (opposite)
LEMON CURD:
Rind of 4 or 5 large
  lemons (colored
  portion only)
1 cup sugar
1 cup freshly
  squeezed lemon
  juice
4 eggs
6 egg yolks
1 cup cold butter, cut
  into pieces

Pinch off walnut-size pieces of dough from the pastry and press each one into a muffin or small tart pan, lining the bottom and side. Trim off the excess.

Mash the lemon rind and sugar in a heavy saucepan. Add the juice, eggs and egg yolks and beat over medium heat until the sugar has dissolved and the mixture is hot. Add the butter a little at a time, beating constantly, and bring the mixture to a boil, about 8 minutes. Strain into a bowl.

Spoon a little curd into each tart and bake in a preheated 375° oven until the pastry is golden, about 15 minutes. Cool briefly, then transfer to a rack.
Makes about 30 tarts

BREADS & QUICK BREADS

Irish Soda Bread

4½ cups all-purpose flour
1 tablespoon baking powder
2 teaspoons salt
1 teaspoon baking soda
3 tablespoons cold butter, cut up
½ cup dried currants
1¼ cups buttermilk
¼ cup cold water

Sift the dry ingredients into a mixing bowl. Cut in the butter until coarsely crumbled, then stir in the currants. Add the buttermilk and water and mix to form a soft dough. Transfer the dough to a lightly floured surface and knead briefly, then shape into a large round about 2 inches thick.

Place on a floured baking sheet, cut a deep cross on top of the loaf and sprinkle with flour. Bake in a preheated 425° oven until the loaf sounds hollow when tapped, about 25 to 30 minutes. Transfer to a rack to cool.
Makes one 8-inch loaf

Raisin Bread

2 packages dry yeast
1¼ cups lukewarm
   milk
¼ cup butter
2 tablespoons honey
4 cups all-purpose
   flour, or more as
   needed
1½ teaspoons salt
¼ cup light brown
   sugar
½ cup dried currants
   or raisins
½ cup golden raisins

Dissolve the yeast in ½ cup of the milk; set aside. To the remaining milk, add the butter and honey, stirring until blended.

Stir together the dry ingredients, currants, raisins, yeast mixture and milk mixture, adding enough flour so that the dough is no longer sticky. Knead until smooth, 5 to 10 minutes. Place in an oiled bowl and let rise in a warm place until doubled in size. Knead briefly; divide in half and place in two greased 9 × 5-inch loaf pans. Cover with a cloth and let rise until the dough reaches the tops of the pans.

Bake in a preheated 375° oven until the loaves sound hollow when tapped, about 35 to 40 minutes. Transfer to a rack, then brush tops with additional honey.

Makes two 9-inch loaves

Whole Wheat Bread

2 packages dry yeast
2 cups lukewarm
   water
3 tablespoons butter
2½ cups whole
   wheat flour
3 cups all-purpose
   flour, or more as
   needed
2 teaspoons salt
2 tablespoons wheat
   germ

Dissolve the yeast in ½ cup of the lukewarm water; set aside for 10 minutes. Melt the butter in the remaining lukewarm water. Mix the flours, salt, yeast and butter mixtures and wheat germ to form a smooth dough.

Knead the dough on a floured surface until smooth and elastic, about 8 to 10 minutes. Place in an oiled bowl, cover with a damp cloth and let rise in a warm place until doubled in size, 1 to 2 hours.

Knead briefly; divide in half. Roll each into a rectangle 9 inches wide. Roll up from one short end and place in a greased 9 × 5-inch loaf pan; repeat with the remaining dough. Brush with water.

Cover and let rise in a warm place until the dough reaches the tops of the pans. Bake in a preheated 425° oven until the loaves sound hollow when tapped, about 30 to 40 minutes. Transfer to a rack to cool.

Makes two 9-inch loaves

Cottage Loaf

2 packages dry yeast
1 teaspoon sugar
2 cups lukewarm
water
6 cups all-purpose
flour
2 teaspoons salt
1 tablespoon
vegetable oil

Combine the yeast, sugar and ½ cup of the lukewarm water; set aside for 10 minutes. Put the flour and salt in a mixing bowl. Make a well in the center; pour in the yeast, remaining water and the oil. Mix well.

Knead the dough on a floured surface until smooth and elastic, 8 to 10 minutes, kneading in more flour if the dough becomes sticky. Place in an oiled bowl, cover with a damp cloth and let rise in a warm place until doubled in size, 1 to 2 hours.

Knead on a floured surface 2 minutes. Divide the dough into two unequal pieces. Shape each piece into a neat round. Place the larger round on a floured baking sheet. Place the smaller round on top and poke a hole in the center. Cover and let rise until nearly doubled in size, about 30 minutes.

Sprinkle with flour and bake in a preheated 425° oven until the loaf sounds hollow when tapped, 35 to 40 minutes. Cool on a rack.

Makes one 2-lb loaf

NOTE: Bake in 2 loaf pans if desired.

Currant Cream Scones

2 cups all-purpose
   flour
1 tablespoon sugar
2 teaspoons baking
   powder
1 teaspoon baking
   soda
½ teaspoon salt
4 tablespoons cold
   butter, cut up
½ cup dried currants
1 egg
1 cup heavy cream

Sift the flour with the sugar, baking powder, baking soda and salt. Cut in the butter until crumbly. Stir in the currants; then make a well in the center. Stir in the egg, lightly beaten with ⅔ cup of the cream. Stir the mixture together with a fork, adding enough cream to make a sticky but manageable dough.

Gently pat out the dough on a floured surface to ¾-inch thickness. Cut out rounds with a 2½-inch fluted cutter and transfer to a greased baking sheet. Brush the tops of the scones with a little cream.

Bake in a preheated 400° oven until lightly golden, 12 to 15 minutes.
Makes about 12 scones

Digestive Biscuits

1¼ cups whole wheat flour

⅓ cup rolled oats (not instant)

½ teaspoon salt

1 teaspoon baking powder

6 tablespoons cold butter

3 tablespoons light brown sugar

3 tablespoons milk, or more as needed

In a bowl, mix together the flour and oats, then mix in the salt and baking powder. Cut in the butter until the mixture is crumbly, then stir in the sugar. Add enough milk to make a stiff but cohesive dough. Roll out thinly on a lightly floured surface and cut into 2½-inch rounds with a plain or fluted cutter. Place the rounds on a greased baking sheet and prick with a fork. Bake in a preheated 375° oven until very lightly browned, about 13 minutes. Transfer to a rack to cool.

Makes about 2 dozen crackers

Long Rye Loaf

2 packages dry yeast
1¼ cups lukewarm
   water
1 tablespoon honey
3 cups all-purpose
   flour
1 cup rye flour
1½ teaspoons salt
1 tablespoon wheat
   germ
1 tablespoon
   vegetable oil
Cracked wheat

Stir together the yeast, ½ cup of the water and the honey; set aside for 15 minutes.

Combine the flours, salt and wheat germ in a bowl and make a well in the center. Stir in the yeast mixture, remaining water and oil and mix to a soft dough.

Knead on a floured surface until smooth and elastic, 5 to 10 minutes. Place in an oiled bowl, cover with a damp cloth and let rise in a warm place until doubled in size, about 1½ hours.

Knead on a floured surface for about 2 minutes. Shape into two long loaves and place on a greased baking sheet. Cut slashes lengthwise along the loaves. Brush with water and sprinkle with the cracked wheat. Cover and let rise until doubled, about 30 minutes.

Bake in a preheated 425° oven until the loaves sound hollow when tapped, about 25 to 30 minutes. Cool on a rack.

Makes 2 long loaves

Herb and Onion Bread

2 packages dry yeast
2 cups lukewarm water
2⅔ cups whole wheat flour
3 cups all-purpose flour
2 teaspoons salt
1 large onion, finely chopped
½ teaspoon dried thyme
1 tablespoon vegetable oil
1 tablespoon sesame seeds

Stir together the yeast and ½ cup of the water and set aside for 15 minutes. Combine with the remaining ingredients, except the sesame seeds, mixing to form a soft but not sticky dough.

Knead on a floured surface until smooth and elastic, about 10 minutes. Place in an oiled bowl, cover with a damp cloth and let rise in a warm place until doubled in size, about 1½ hours. Punch down the dough.

Knead on a floured surface for 2 minutes. Form into two round loaves and place on a greased baking sheet. Brush with water and sprinkle with the sesame seeds. Cover the loaves with a damp cloth and let rise in a warm place until nearly doubled in size, about 30 minutes.

Bake in a preheated 425° oven for 15 minutes. Lower the heat to 375° and bake until the loaves sound hollow when tapped, about 15 to 20 minutes longer. Cool on a rack.

Makes 2 round loaves

Cheese and Bacon Bread

3 slices bacon, diced
1 small onion, finely chopped
2 cups all-purpose flour
2 teaspoons baking powder
1 teaspoon salt
Pinch of pepper
4 tablespoons cold butter
1 cup grated sharp Cheddar cheese
2 eggs
⅔ cup milk
1 teaspoon Dijon mustard
1 tablespoon chopped parsley

Cook the bacon in a skillet until lightly golden; drain on paper towels. Add the onion to the skillet and cook until soft, 5 to 7 minutes. Add to the bacon.

Sift the flour, baking powder and salt into a bowl. Add the pepper and cut in the butter until the mixture is crumbly. Stir in the cheese and the bacon and onion.

Beat together the eggs, milk, mustard and parsley; add to the dry ingredients and beat thoroughly.

Transfer the mixture to a greased 9 × 5-inch loaf pan and bake in a preheated 375° oven until firm and golden, about 45 minutes. Leave in the pan for 5 minutes, then cool on a rack.

Makes one 9-inch loaf

Biscuit Ring

2 cups all-purpose flour
2 teaspoons baking powder
1 teaspoon salt
1 teaspoon dry mustard
3 tablespoons cold butter
1 cup grated sharp Cheddar cheese
2 tablespoons chopped chives or parsley
⅔ to ¾ cup milk
Beaten egg

Sift the flour, baking powder, salt and mustard into a bowl. Cut in the butter until the mixture is crumbly. Stir in the cheese, chives and milk to form a soft, slightly sticky dough.

Knead very briefly on a lightly floured surface. Roll out to ½-inch thickness. Use a plain or fluted cutter to cut out 8 biscuits. Arrange them in a ring, overlapping slightly, on a greased baking sheet. Brush with the beaten egg. Bake in a preheated 425° oven until golden, about 15 minutes. Transfer to a rack to cool slightly.

Serve warm. Split open each biscuit and spread with butter.

Makes 8 biscuits

Banana-Pecan Bread

½ cup light brown
   sugar, packed
3 tablespoons
   granulated sugar
⅓ cup vegetable oil
2 eggs, lightly beaten
1¾ cups all-purpose
   flour
2 teaspoons baking
   powder
½ teaspoon salt
¼ teaspoon baking
   soda
½ teaspoon allspice
3 ripe bananas,
   mashed
¾ cup coarsely
   chopped pecans

Beat the sugars and oil until blended;
add the eggs and beat until smooth. Sift
together the dry ingredients and add to
the sugar mixture, beating. Fold in the
bananas and pecans.

Pour the batter into a greased 9 ×
5-inch loaf pan. Bake in a preheated
350° oven until set, about 1 hour. Cool
briefly in the pan, then transfer to a
rack to cool completely.
Makes one 9-inch loaf

Cranberry Nut Bread

2 cups all-purpose
  flour
1 cup sugar
1 teaspoon baking
  soda
1 teaspoon cream of
  tartar
½ teaspoon
  cinnamon
¼ teaspoon salt
1 egg, lightly beaten
¾ cup orange juice
3 tablespoons
  vegetable oil
Grated rind of 1 large
  orange
2 cups chopped fresh
  cranberries
½ cup chopped
  walnuts or pecans

Sift together the flour, sugar, baking soda, cream of tartar, cinnamon and salt. Stir together the egg, orange juice, vegetable oil and orange rind. Stir together the dry and moist ingredients, just until partially blended. Fold in the cranberries and nuts until blended.

Spoon the batter into a greased 9 × 5-inch loaf pan, spreading evenly. Bake in a preheated 350° oven until the center is set, 50 to 60 minutes. Transfer to a rack to cool.

Makes one 9-inch loaf

Peanut and Cheese Wafers

½ cup all-purpose
  flour
¾ teaspoon baking
  powder
½ teaspoon baking
  soda
¼ teaspoon salt
⅓ cup whole wheat
  flour
2 tablespoons cold
  butter
2 tablespoons
  chunky peanut
  butter
1 cup grated sharp
  Cheddar cheese
¼ cup chopped
  salted peanuts
1 egg, lightly beaten
Milk, if needed

Sift the flour, baking powder, baking
soda and salt into a bowl. Stir in the
whole wheat flour. Cut in the butter
and peanut butter until the mixture is
crumbly. Stir in the cheese and
peanuts. Add the egg and enough milk
to hold the mixture together.

Knead the dough once or twice on a
lightly floured surface until smooth.
Roll out to ¼-inch thickness and cut
out 2-inch rounds, using a plain or
fluted cutter. Place on a greased baking
sheet.

Bake in a preheated 375° oven until
lightly browned, about 10 to 15 minutes. Cool on a rack.

Makes about 2 dozen wafers

Cottage Cheese Date Bread

2 cups all-purpose
   flour
1½ teaspoons
   baking powder
¼ teaspoon baking
   soda
Pinch of salt
¼ teaspoon each
   nutmeg and
   allspice
2 tablespoons sugar
4 tablespoons cold
   butter
2 eggs
½ cup cottage
   cheese
¼ cup milk
3 tablespoons
   chopped walnuts
½ cup chopped
   pitted dates

Sift the flour, baking powder, baking soda, salt and spices into a bowl. Stir in the sugar; cut in the butter until the mixture is crumbly. Beat the eggs with the cheese and milk; then add to the dry ingredients with the walnuts and dates. Mix well.

Pour the batter into a greased 9 × 5-inch loaf pan. Bake in a preheated 350° oven until risen and golden, about 45 minutes. Leave in the pan briefly; then transfer to a rack to cool. Serve sliced, with sweet butter.

Makes one 9-inch loaf

Biscuit Round

2 cups all-purpose
flour
2 tablespoons sugar
1 tablespoon baking
powder
½ teaspoon baking
soda
½ teaspoon salt
5 tablespoons cold
butter
⅓ cup golden raisins
½ cup buttermilk, or
more as needed
Milk to glaze

Sift the flour, sugar, baking powder, baking soda and salt into a bowl; cut in the butter until crumbly. Stir in the raisins and enough buttermilk to make a slightly sticky dough.

Knead gently on a floured surface, then form into a 7-inch round and place on a greased baking sheet.

Score the round into 8 sections and brush with milk. Bake in a preheated 400° oven until golden brown, about 20 to 30 minutes. Transfer to a rack to cool; serve with butter and jam.

Makes one 7-inch round

Whole Wheat Biscuits

1½ cups all-purpose
flour
1 tablespoon baking
powder
1 teaspoon salt
½ teaspoon baking
soda
½ cup whole wheat
flour
5 tablespoons cold
butter, cut up
1 egg, lightly beaten
½ cup buttermilk, or
as needed
1 tablespoon honey
Beaten egg to glaze

Sift together the all-purpose flour, baking powder, salt and baking soda. Stir in the whole wheat flour, then cut in the butter until crumbly. Make a well in the center and pour in the egg, buttermilk and honey. Stir with a fork, adding buttermilk if needed, to form a sticky but manageable dough.

Pat the dough on a floured surface to a ¾-inch thickness. Cut out 2-inch rounds and transfer to a greased baking sheet. Repeat with the remaining dough. Brush the rounds with beaten egg. Bake in a preheated 400° oven until golden, about 16 minutes. Cool on a rack. Serve with butter and jam.

Makes 12 biscuits

Cheese-Topped Biscuits

2 cups all-purpose
 flour
2 teaspoons baking
 powder
1 teaspoon dry
 mustard
½ teaspoon salt
Pinch of cayenne
 pepper
5 tablespoons cold
 butter
1 cup grated Swiss
 cheese
1 egg, beaten
¼ cup milk, or more
 as needed
Milk to glaze

Sift the flour, baking powder, mustard, salt and cayenne into a bowl; cut in the butter until the mixture is crumbly. Stir in most of the cheese, the egg and enough milk to make a soft dough.

Roll out the dough on a floured surface to ¾-inch thickness. Cut into 2-inch rounds with a plain or fluted cutter and transfer to a greased baking sheet. Brush with milk and sprinkle with the remaining cheese.

Bake in a preheated 400° oven until golden, about 15 minutes. Transfer to a rack to cool. Serve warm, with butter.
Makes about 12 biscuits

87

Cinnamon-Raisin Buns

RICH YEAST DOUGH:
1 package dry yeast
⅓ cup lukewarm milk
¼ cup sugar
2 cups all-purpose flour
½ teaspoon salt
¼ cup butter, melted
1 egg, lightly beaten
FILLING:
4 tablespoons butter, melted
¼ cup light brown sugar, packed
½ cup raisins
½ teaspoon cinnamon
¼ teaspoon allspice
GLAZE:
3 tablespoons sugar, boiled with 3 tablespoons water for 2 minutes

Stir together the yeast, milk and sugar; set aside for 15 minutes. Sift the flour and salt into a bowl, make a well in the center and add the yeast mixture, butter and egg; mix until smooth. Knead on a floured surface until very smooth, 5 to 10 minutes. Place in an oiled bowl; cover and let rise until doubled in size. Knead for 2 minutes, then roll out to a 9 × 12-inch rectangle.

To fill, brush the dough with melted butter, then sprinkle with the sugar, raisins and spices. Roll up from one short end. Cut into 9 slices and lay flat in a greased 8-inch square pan.

Cover and let rise until nearly doubled, about 20 minutes. Bake in a preheated 400° oven until golden, about 20 to 25 minutes. Brush with glaze immediately.

Makes 9 buns

Maple-Walnut Muffins

1½ cups all-purpose flour
1 tablespoon baking powder
¾ teaspoon salt
1 tablespoon brown sugar
½ cup whole wheat flour
½ cup coarsely chopped walnuts
2 eggs
¾ cup milk
⅓ cup maple syrup
¼ cup butter, melted

Sift the all-purpose flour, baking powder and salt into a bowl; stir in the sugar, whole wheat flour and walnuts. Make a well in the center.

Stir together the eggs, milk, maple syrup and butter until blended. Pour into the well and quickly stir the ingredients together *just* until the flour is moistened, no longer.

Spoon the batter into well-greased muffin pans and bake in a preheated 400° oven until muffins are lightly browned, about 20 minutes. Serve warm.

Makes 12 muffins

Sally Lunn

2 packages dry yeast
⅔ cup lukewarm
   milk
¼ cup sugar
3 cups all-purpose
   flour
1 egg, lightly beaten
Finely grated rind of
   1 lemon
6 tablespoons butter
Beaten egg

Stir together the yeast, milk, 1 tea-spoon of the sugar and 2 tablespoons of the flour; set aside for 15 minutes.

Sift the remaining flour into a bowl, make a well in the center and add the yeast mixture, remaining sugar and the egg and lemon rind. Mix vigorous-ly until smooth. Work in the butter and mix well. Knead for 2 minutes and shape into a ball. Place the dough in a greased bowl, cover with a towel and let rise in a warm place until doubled in size.

Divide the dough in half and shape each into a ball. Place on a baking sheet or in two small greased cake pans. Cover and let rise in a warm place for 30 to 40 minutes.

Brush the loaves gently with the beaten egg. Bake in a preheated 425° oven until golden brown, about 20 minutes. Cool on a rack. Serve warm or at room temperature with butter and jam.

Makes 2 loaves

Bath Buns

Sally Lunn dough
   (above)
½ cup golden raisins
Finely grated rind of
   2 lemons
¼ cup crushed sugar
   cubes
Beaten egg

Prepare the Sally Lunn dough and let rise in the bowl as directed.

Add the raisins, lemon rind and half of the sugar to the dough and knead until blended.

Shape the dough into 16 roughly-shaped buns and place on a greased baking sheet, spacing well apart. Cov-er and let rise for 20 minutes. Brush lightly with the beaten egg and sprin-kle with the remaining. Bake in a preheated 425° oven until golden, 10 to 15 minutes. Cool on a rack; serve with sweet butter.

Makes 16 buns

BASIC RECIPES

Basic Pie Pastry

1¼ cups all-purpose flour
1 teaspoon sugar
¼ teaspoon salt
5 tablespoons cold butter, cut up
2 tablespoons cold shortening, cut up
2 tablespoons cold water, or more as needed

Sift the flour, sugar and salt into a bowl. Cut in the butter and shortening until the mixture is crumbly. Add just enough cold water until the pastry can be gathered into a ball. Knead once or twice, then gather into a ball, wrap in plastic wrap and chill at least 1 hour.
Makes pastry for a 9- or 10-inch one-crust pie

Rich Tart Pastry

1½ cups all-purpose flour
2 tablespoons sugar
Pinch of salt
½ cup cold butter, cut up
1 egg yolk
1 tablespoon cold water, or more as needed

Sift the flour, sugar and salt into a large bowl. Cut in the butter until crumbly.

Stir together the egg yolk and water, then stir into the flour mixture with a fork. Add just enough cold water until the pastry can be gathered into a ball. Knead gently once or twice, then gather into a ball, wrap in plastic wrap and chill at least 1 hour.
Makes pastry for a 9- or 10-inch one-crust pie

Pastry Cream

1¼ cups milk
3 egg yolks
½ cup sugar
¼ cup flour
1 teaspoon vanilla
1 tablespoon butter

Bring the milk to a boil. Meanwhile, in a bowl, beat together the egg yolks, sugar and flour. Gradually beat the hot milk into the mixture. Return the mixture to the pan and bring to a boil, beating. Boil 1 minute; strain into a bowl and stir in the vanilla and butter. Place a piece of plastic wrap on the custard surface and cool. Will keep for 1 week if not disturbed.
Makes about 2 cups

Quick Buttercream

1 lb butter
1 cup sifted
   powdered sugar
1 to 2 egg whites
1 teaspoon vanilla or
   other flavoring

In a food processor or electric mixer, beat the butter until very light and smooth, at least 2 minutes. Add the sugar and beat again until fluffy, at least 2 minutes. Add the egg white, beating until smooth. Add the flavoring to taste.
Makes enough to fill and frost one 9-inch layer cake

Ganache

½ cup heavy cream
8 oz semisweet
   chocolate, cut up
   coarsely

Heat the cream in a heavy saucepan until nearly boiling. Add the chocolate and stir over moderate heat until melted and completely smooth. Cool slightly to use as a pouring glaze; chill if a firm consistency is desired or if using for truffles.
Makes enough to glaze one large cake

Sugar Syrup

2 cups water
1 lb sugar

Combine the water and sugar in a heavy-bottomed saucepan and bring to a boil over high heat. Wash down the side of the pan with a pastry brush dipped in cold water; boil for 2 minutes. Remove from the heat and cool. Store in the refrigerator.
Makes about 2 cups

INDEX